Military Police

by Michael Green

3370900499209

Consultant:
Richard H. Marty
Major, MP
United States Army Reserve

CAPSTONE BOOKS
an imprint of Capstone Press
Mankato, Minnesota

Capstone Books are published by Capstone Press
151 Good Counsel Drive, P.O. Box 669, Mankato, Minnesota 56002
http://www.capstone-press.com

Library of Congress Cataloging-in-Publication Data
Green, Michael, 1952–
    Military police/by Michael Green.
    p. cm.—(Serving your country)
    Includes bibliographical references and index.
    Summary: Discusses the history, duties, training, and equipment of the U.S. Army
military police.
    ISBN 0-7368-0473-0
    1. United States. Army—Military police—Juvenile literature. [1. United States.
Army—Military police—Vocational guidance. 2. Vocational guidance.] I. Title.
II. Series.
UB825.U54 G74 2000
355.1'3323—dc21   99-053872

Editorial Credits

Matt Doeden, editor; Timothy Halldin, cover designer; Linda Clavel, production designer;
    Heidi Schoof, photo researcher

Photo Credits

Andrew Rakoczy/FPG International LLC, 19
Defense Visual Information Center, cover
Michael Green, 27
National Archives, 12, 15, 16
Photri-Microstock, 8, 11, 36, 39, 40, 43
Unicorn Stock Photos, 32
U.S. Army, 4, 7, 20, 23, 24, 28, 30, 35

1 2 3 4 5 6 05 04 03 02 01 00

Table of Contents

Chapter 1
Military Police

Military police (MPs) are the police force of
the U.S. military. MPs are U.S. Army members
with special training in law enforcement. Other
branches of the military also have specialized
law enforcement groups. But MPs are the
largest law enforcement group in the military.

MPs perform four basic missions. They are
in charge of battlefield circulation control
(BCC) and area security. MPs also handle
enemy prisoners of war (EPW) operations and
law and order operations.

MPs are the military's police force.

Battlefield Circulation Control

MPs perform BCC during combat. MPs operate from the rear of combat areas. They direct troop units and vehicles. They make sure each troop unit and vehicle driver knows where to go. MPs may form checkpoints on roads to make sure people do not enter certain areas. MPs also prevent U.S. soldiers from leaving their combat posts without permission. Soldiers who leave their battle posts are called deserters.

MPs sometimes guard convoys from enemy attacks. A convoy is a group of military vehicles that carries supplies or troops. MPs make sure convoys reach their destinations safely.

MPs also serve as infantry soldiers when needed. Infantry soldiers fight in ground combat. MPs often fight from the rear of a combat area. They use weapons such as machine guns and grenade launchers. MPs use these weapons to fight enemy troops and to destroy enemy vehicles.

MPs may form checkpoints on roads to make sure people do not enter certain areas.

MPs who perform area security guard buildings and areas.

Area Security

Area security is another important MP mission. MPs who perform area security guard a variety of buildings and areas. These include military bases, hospitals, storage areas, and missile silos. The U.S. military stores its large missiles at these silos.

MPs who perform security duties make sure only authorized people enter certain areas. For example, only high-ranking officers may be allowed to enter rooms where battle plans are made. MPs may check passes or identification cards of people who try to enter such areas.

MPs may make sure no one brings weapons into certain areas. They may use metal detectors to search people for weapons. Metal detectors have sensors that indicate when metal objects pass through gates. These sensors detect guns, knives, and some explosives. MPs may take away weapons from people who try to enter secure areas. MPs also may arrest people who try to bring weapons into these areas.

EPW Operations

During wartime, MPs guard enemy prisoners of war (EPWs). These enemy soldiers are captured during combat. MPs may have to set up temporary holding areas when prisons are not available. They also may have to transport EPWs to military prisons. MPs prevent EPWs from escaping. MPs also prevent civilians and soldiers from harming EPWs.

MPs in military prisons perform many of the same duties as civilian prison guards. A civilian is someone who is not in the military. MPs keep order inside prisons. They also perform area security at military prisons. They make sure prisoners do not escape.

Law and Order Operations

MPs perform the U.S. military's law and order operations. They make sure members of the military obey laws. MPs arrest members who do not. MPs also must be ready to provide civilian law enforcement. They may take over for civilian police departments during disasters or other emergencies.

MPs also oversee the Criminal Investigation Division (CID). This group includes military detectives. Detectives gather information on crimes. They sometimes testify in court regarding their investigations.

MPs sometimes take over for civilian police departments during emergencies.

Chapter 2
History

The United States first used military police during the Revolutionary War (1775–1783). At that time, the United States was fighting for its independence from Great Britain. General George Washington helped create the Provost Corps during the war. This unit of soldiers oversaw enemy prisoners. Provost Corps members also tracked and arrested enemy spies and U.S. deserters.

The United States disbanded the Provost Corps after the Revolutionary War. It did not form another military police force for almost 80 years.

The Provost Corps was the first U.S. group of military police.

Military Police Return

The United States needed another military police force during the Civil War (1861–1865). Eleven Southern states left the United States during this war. They formed the Confederate States of America. The United States fought to restore the Confederate States to the nation. The U.S. Army started a military police force called the Veteran Reserve Corps. This force's mission was to make civilians fight for the United States. The Army disbanded this group when the Civil War ended.

The U.S. military formed a new military police force near the end of World War I (1914–1918). This group was called the MP Corps. The MP Corps existed for only about one year. The military disbanded the MP Corps after World War I ended.

Some military officials felt the Army needed a permanent force of MPs. In 1921, the Army trained some soldiers to be MPs. These soldiers were similar to today's MPs. They wore a special insignia on their uniforms. This

MPs guarded many Japanese soldiers taken as prisoners during World War II.

badge included two crossed Harpers Ferry pistols. This insignia identified the MPs to other soldiers.

World War II

In 1941, the United States entered World War II (1939–1945). The United States and the Allied forces fought the Axis powers during this war. The Allied forces included the United

MPs guarded railroads during World War II.

Kingdom, Canada, Russia, and France. The Axis powers included Germany, Japan, and Italy.

The U.S. Army formed the Corps of Military Police to maintain order during World War II. The Corps of Military Police performed many duties. It watched over the many new soldiers entering the military. It made sure the new soldiers followed rules and laws. The Corps of Military Police also guarded thousands of EPWs. The United States held more than 400,000 EPWs by the end of World War II. The Corps of Military Police guarded prisons that held these EPWs.

The Corps of Military Police also was important during World War II combat. MPs directed traffic. They made sure military vehicles went to the proper locations. MPs provided protection and transportation to important military officers. Many MPs also fought in battles alongside infantry soldiers.

The Army learned how valuable MPs were during wartime. The military trained more soldiers to be MPs. The Corps of Military Police started with about 2,000 members. By 1945, it had more than 200,000 members.

After World War II
In 1945, the Allied forces defeated the Axis powers. U.S. MPs remained in defeated enemy countries after World War II. They enforced laws

and kept order in these countries. MPs also prevented new military groups from forming.

By 1950, the Army's MP force had dropped to about 20,000 members. The United States then became involved in the Korean War (1950–1953). North Korea and South Korea fought each other during this war. Both sides wanted Korea to be one country. But each side wanted a different kind of government. The United States supported South Korea in this war. The Army needed more MPs to assist its war efforts. The military decided to make MPs a permanent part of the Army.

By 1951, the Army's MP force had grown to more than 40,000 members. These MPs performed many duties during the Korean War. The war left many South Korean civilians homeless. They became refugees. MPs helped to control the many refugees in the area. MPs also went on patrols for enemy troops. They tracked down and arrested spies. MPs also guarded important locations such as bridges and tunnels.

MPs played an important role in the Vietnam War.

The Vietnam War

MPs played an important role in the Vietnam War (1954–1975). The U.S. military fought alongside the South Vietnamese military during this war. They fought against the North Vietnamese military. Both sides wanted all of Vietnam to be one country. But each side wanted a different kind of government.

The Vietnam War included a great deal of guerrilla warfare. Guerrilla warriors fight in small groups behind enemy lines. North Vietnamese guerrillas often attacked U.S. military posts. The attacks were hard to predict. MPs guarded important locations and officials from these surprise attacks.

By 1968, the U.S. military had more than 500,000 troops in Vietnam. About 30,000 of these were MPs. The U.S. military used truck convoys to bring supplies to its troops. MPs protected these convoys. Teams of MPs operated armored vehicles to make sure the convoys reached their destinations safely. Armored vehicles have thick armor that protects the vehicles from most weapon fire.

MPs in the 1990s

On August 2, 1990, Iraq's military invaded the nearby country of Kuwait. Iraqi leaders wanted control of oil wells in Kuwait. The U.S. military sent troops to stop the invasion. This led to the Gulf War (1991).

MPs patrolled areas near U.S. bases during the Gulf War.

The U.S. military sent almost 20,000 MPs to the Gulf War. These MPs performed military traffic control, guarded important sites, and prepared EPW camps.

On February 23, 1991, the U.S. Army attacked the Iraqi military. MP units followed Army combat units into battle. Army soldiers captured more than 5,000 Iraqi soldiers in less than 10 hours. Later, more than 80,000 Iraqi soldiers surrendered to the U.S. military. MPs handled and controlled all of these EPWs.

Some MPs stayed in Kuwait after the Gulf War. They helped maintain order in Kuwait until civilian police regained control of the country.

MPs went to the African country of Somalia during the early 1990s. Somalia was under the control of criminal warlords at this time. Many Somalian people were starving and sick because of the warlords' actions. The United States sent relief workers to help Somalia's people. MPs protected these workers from the warlords. MPs guarded supply docks and

MPs guarded important locations during the Gulf War.

supply centers. They also guarded truck convoys that brought food and other supplies to the Somalian people.

In 1996, about 1,400 MPs went to the European nation of Bosnia. People of different ethnic and religious groups were fighting one another there. MPs tried to help keep order in Bosnia. They tried to stop Bosnian people from fighting one another.

Chapter 3
Vehicles and Equipment

Mps use a variety of equipment and vehicles to perform their duties. MPs carry weapons to control prisoners and to protect civilians. They use armored vehicles to transport important officers and officials.

Weapons
The M-9 pistol is the most common MP weapon. The M-9 is lightweight and easy to use. It is a semiautomatic pistol. Semiautomatic weapons fire one bullet each

MPs carry weapons to protect civilians and themselves.

time the trigger is pulled. M-9s can hold up to 16 bullets.

MPs in combat areas frequently carry M-16 rifles. These weapons are heavier and more powerful than pistols. They hold up to 30 bullets. M-16s can fire up to three bullets with each squeeze of the trigger.

MP crews in combat areas also may use machine guns. These large, automatic weapons can fire many bullets in a short period of time. Automatic weapons can fire more than one bullet when the trigger is pulled. The M-2 is a common MP machine gun. MPs must mount the M-2 onto a tripod to fire it. This stand has three legs that hold the machine gun steady. MPs also use the Squad Automatic Weapon (SAW). This machine gun is lighter and easier to use than the M-2.

MPs also may use Mark 19 grenade launchers. These weapons fire small explosives long distances. MPs use Mark 19s to attack enemy troops or vehicles. A Mark 19's grenade can damage targets within 57 feet (17 meters) of its explosion.

MPs sometimes use Mark 19 grenade launchers during combat.

Armored Vehicles

MPs sometimes use armored vehicles to transport supplies, troops, and officials. They also use armored cars to patrol roads near military posts. Armored vehicles sometimes are armed with guns.

MPs use a variety of armored vehicles. Some are large tanks. These slow vehicles have thick layers of armor. Other armored

vehicles include jeeps and cars, and trucks called Humvees. These vehicles have thinner armor. But they are faster than heavy tanks.

Other Equipment

MPs need other kinds of equipment to do their jobs. They use handcuffs to restrain prisoners. They may defend themselves with wooden clubs called batons. MPs use radar to track the speed and direction of ground vehicles. They use radios to communicate.

MPs sometimes need extra safety equipment. They may wear helmets and bulletproof clothing to protect themselves from attack. Bulletproof clothing stops some kinds of bullets from entering the body. They may wear gas masks and protective suits to protect themselves from chemical attacks.

MPs carry radios to communicate with one another.

Machine Gunner

Radio Antenna

Storage Space

Humvee Armored Vehicle

Chapter 4
Training

MPs receive special training. People who want to become MPs must first become U.S. Army officers or enlisted members. Officers have higher ranks than enlisted members. Officers supervise enlisted members.

Enlisted members and officers who wish to become MPs must complete MP training. This training teaches them how to perform MP duties.

Enlisted Training
All enlisted members of the Army begin their careers in basic training. They are called privates. This is the lowest rank in the Army.

Recruits spend eight weeks in basic training.

Privates must complete eight weeks of basic training.

Drill sergeants make privates work hard during basic training. Privates wake up early and train until late in the day. They do exercises. They go on long runs and marches. Privates learn about weapons and practice using them. They also learn about military rules and laws.

Most privates receive specialist training after basic training. Privates who wish to be MPs must complete six weeks of specialist training. This training is conducted at the MP School at Fort Leonard Wood, Missouri.

Trainees at the MP School learn a variety of law-enforcement skills. They learn to perform many of the duties civilian law-enforcement officers perform. For example, trainees learn to write traffic tickets. They also learn how to control prisoners. Trainees practice setting up temporary holding areas. MP trainees also learn how to control crowds. They must understand how to handle large groups of

At MP school, trainees learn how to set up temporary holding areas.

panicked civilians. MPs may need to do this to maintain order during emergencies.

Enlisted members earn higher ranks as they serve and receive more training. The highest rank an enlisted member can hold is sergeant major. Enlisted members can become officers by receiving a bachelor's degree from a college or university. Members must also complete additional training to become officers.

Officer Training

Officers can train for their Army service in several ways. Some college students prepare for careers in the Army by attending Reserve Officer Training Corps (ROTC) programs. College graduates may become officers by completing Officer Candidate School (OCS). At this school, students learn about the Army and how to be leaders. Some students become officers by attending the U.S. Military Academy. They must complete four years of education and training there.

Some students become officers by attending the U.S. Military Academy.

Officers who want to become MPs must receive additional training. They must complete a six-month course at MP School. They learn how to perform basic law enforcement tasks at this school. They learn many of the same skills enlisted MPs learn. Officers also learn to make decisions and give orders to other MPs.

Most officers enter the Army as second lieutenants. Officers who enter the Army with specialized training may enter at higher ranks. Experienced doctors or lawyers may enter as captains. Officers can earn higher ranks with experience and training. The highest rank an officer can reach is general.

General is the highest rank an officer can reach.

Chapter 5

The Future

Some military officials believe large conflicts like the Vietnam War will be rare in the future. Many of these officials believe that urban warfare and terrorism will become bigger problems. These kinds of warfare often occur in cities. U.S. citizens may be at risk in these situations. MPs and soldiers learn to use their weapons in heavily populated areas. They also must learn to control large groups of frightened civilians.

MPs may perform more peacekeeping missions in the future. The governments of

MPs must know how to control large groups of people.

other countries sometimes cannot control their citizens. These governments may ask the United States for help. The U.S. military may send MPs to help control these citizens. MPs can stop dangerous riots and help bring order back to these countries.

New Equipment

The military is designing a new armored vehicle called the Armored Security Vehicle (ASV). MPs will be able to use the ASV in urban areas. The ASV will protect its crew from most types of enemy fire. The ASV will be armed with grenade launchers and machine guns.

MPs also are learning to use computers to help them perform their duties. Computers help MPs in a variety of ways. MPs can use computers to keep detailed records of prisoners and military personnel. They also can use computer simulations to prepare for disasters. Computer simulations are models

MPs may perform more peacekeeping missions in the future.

that show MPs how disasters might affect different areas. Disasters may include earthquakes, hurricanes, and outbreaks of deadly diseases. Simulations help MPs and other military personnel prepare to save lives when disasters occur.

Words to Know

civilian (si-VIL-yuhn)—a person who is not in the military

convoy (KON-voi)—a formation of military vehicles traveling together

deserter (di-ZUR-tuhr)—a soldier who leaves a combat post without permission

infantry (IN-fuhn-tree)—soldiers trained to fight on the ground

insignia (in-SIG-nee-uh)—a badge or emblem used to mark membership in a military organization

mission (MISH-uhn)—a military task

radar (RAY-dar)—machinery that uses radio waves to locate and guide objects

refugee (ref-yuh-JEE)—a person who is forced to leave his or her home because of a war or natural disaster

tripod (TRYE-pod)—a three-legged stand; MPs use tripods to hold machine guns steady.

To Learn More

Green, Michael. *The United States Army.* Serving Your Country. Mankato, Minn.: Capstone Books, 1998.

Smith, Jay H. *Humvees and Other Military Vehicles.* Wheels. Minneapolis: Capstone Books, 1995.

Useful Addresses

Military Police School
Director of Training, MANSCEN
Fort Leonard Wood, MO 65473

U.S. Army Public Affairs
1500 Army Pentagon
Washington, DC 20310-1500

Internet Sites

U.S. Army
http://www.army.mil

U.S. Army Military Police Corps Regiment
http://www.wood.army.mil/usamps/default.htm

U.S. Army Military Police History
http://www.azstarnet.com/~rovedo/mphist.html

Index